# EXTINCT REPTILES

## and those in danger of extinction

## Philip Steele

**Franklin Watts**
London New York Sydney Toronto

© 1991 Zoe Books Limited

Devised and produced by
Zoe Books Limited
15 Worthy Lane
Winchester
Hampshire SO23 7AB
England

First published in 1991
in Great Britain by
Franklin Watts Ltd
96 Leonard Street
London EC2A 4RH

First published in Australia by
Franklin Watts Australia
14 Mars Road
Lane Cove
New South Wales 2066

ISBN 0 7496 0529 4

A CIP catalogue record for this book is
available from the British Library.

Printed in the United Kingdom

Consultant: Professor Richard T. J. Moody,
BSc, Dip Ed, PhD, FGS.
Design: Julian Holland Publishing Ltd
Picture researcher: Jennifer Johnson
Illustrator: Robert Morton

**Photograph acknowledgements**
p10 Michael Freeman/Bruce Coleman Ltd,
p15 Heather Angel, 17 Hans Reinhard/
Bruce Coleman Ltd, p18 Robert P Carr/
Bruce Coleman Ltd, p19 Soames
Summerhays/Biofotos, p20 Christian
Zuber/Bruce Coleman Ltd, p21 Alan
Power/Bruce Coleman Ltd, p22 Frank
Lane Picture Agency, p23 Francisco Erize/
Bruce Coleman Ltd, p24 Michael P Price/
Bruce Coleman Ltd, p25 Joanna Van
Gruisen/Ardea, p26 Alan Compost/Bruce
Coleman Ltd, p27 Robert Quest.

# Contents

# Rodriguez tortoises

Three hundred years ago, the islands in the Indian Ocean swarmed with giant tortoises. They were slow, harmless creatures that lumbered along in the warm sunshine. One visitor to the island of Rodriguez said that he saw as many as 2000 to 3000 tortoises together at one time.

Today, there are no giant tortoises on Rodriguez. They have become extinct. During the seventeenth century the islands were visited by pirates and by Dutch sailors, who discovered that the tortoises were good to eat. In the following century, French and British sailing ships often stopped at Rodriguez so that the sailors could find fresh food and water. They killed the tortoises in vast numbers. Traders took thousands of the tortoises each year to feed people on nearby islands, such as Mauritius. On other islands in the Indian and Pacific Oceans tortoises were killed for food, and many species of giant tortoise became extinct.

DID YOU KNOW?
- The largest tortoise ever known lived between 12 and 7 million years ago. Its shell was 2.2 m (86 in) long and it weighed 955 kg (2105 lb).
- Living reptiles, like the crocodile, the marine turtle and the lizard, are distant relatives of the dinosaurs, which have been extinct for 65 million years.
- There are about 6000 species of reptiles surviving in the world today.

c1700  Two species of giant tortoise extinct on Mauritius.
c1733  Two species of giant tortoise extinct on Réunion.
1795  The last two giant tortoises recorded on Rodriguez.

▲ The Rodriguez Greater Saddleback Tortoise (right) was 85 cm (34 in) long, and had a shell that was raised at the front. This allowed it to feed on tall plants. The Rodriguez Lesser Tortoise (left) was 42 cm (17 in) long, and had a low, arched shell. It fed on grasses at ground level.

WHAT IS A REPTILE?
- Tortoises, snakes, lizards and crocodiles are all reptiles.
- Reptiles are cold-blooded. This means that they cannot control their body temperature, which changes according to the temperature of the air around them. Reptiles need to bask in the sun to gain warmth.
- The bodies of reptiles are covered in scales or horny plates.
- Most reptiles lay eggs which hatch into young. However, there are some reptiles, such as vipers, that give birth to live young.

# Giant lizards

Over six million years, the Earth has gone through many changes. After plants and animals appeared on the planet, species had to adapt if the climate or their food source changed. They had to develop or evolve. Otherwise they became extinct.

The first reptiles developed about 340 million years ago. Reptiles breathe air, and mostly live on land, although some, like sea snakes and crocodiles, spend most of their time in the water.

Reptiles such as the dinosaurs roamed the planet for millions of years. Huge species evolved, many with armour-plated bodies, horns or spiky tails. These enormous reptiles are also known as "terrible lizards". Some were fierce meat-eaters, that hunted other dinosaurs, while others were large, lumbering plant-eaters.

About 65 million years ago, the dinosaurs became extinct. Nobody knows why. It is possible that a sudden change in the climate killed many of the plants on which the larger dinosaurs fed. The meat-eating dinosaurs would in turn have had no food.

▶ One of the largest meat-eaters was called *Tyrannosaurus rex,* or "king tyrant-lizard". This ferocious dinosaur stood 5.6 m (18 ft) high, weighed up to 7 tonnes (7 tons) and measured 14.3 m (47 ft) from nose to tail. It had massive teeth and sharp claws with which it killed other dinosaurs. Remains of *Tyrannosaurus* were first discovered in 1902, in the North American state of Montana.

DID YOU KNOW?
- *Tyrannosaurus* had a skull that was 1.2 m (4 ft) long. Its saw-edged teeth measured 15 cm (6 in) from tip to root.
- *Tyrannosaurus* probably used its weak front legs to help raise itself from the ground after it had been resting.

340 million years ago: First reptiles evolve.
75 million years ago: *Tyrannosaurus rex* stalks the Earth.
65 million years ago: Dinosaurs become extinct.

# Uncovering the past

How do we know about animals that lived long before humans existed? Creatures like mammals and reptiles, which have bony skeletons, have left behind remains called fossils. Long ago, the bodies of dead reptiles were buried in mud, tar or volcanic ash. As the weight of new layers of mud, tar or ash pressed down on the remains, the soft parts were usually destroyed but the bones survived. The bones and teeth were preserved in stone.

By digging up and examining the fossils, scientists can work out how extinct animals once lived. Fossils of previously unknown reptiles are often discovered, and each one adds to our knowledge of the past.

▼ *Rhamphorhynchus* was a flying reptile that lived about 150 million years ago. It measured up to 50 cm (20 in) in length. From remains found in southern Germany, scientists can tell that it had leathery wings, and, unlike most reptiles, a hairy body. Its long tail helped it to steer when flying. The long snout was packed with spiky teeth that scientists think it used for eating fish.

▲ *Elasmosaurus* was a huge reptile, 13 m (43 ft) long. Over half its length was taken up by its long, snake-like neck. *Elasmosaurus* swam in the seas which, 80 million years ago, covered the land that is now the North American state of Kansas. Its small, blunt snout was packed with long, sharp teeth. These were used to grasp the slippery fish that were its daily diet.

DID YOU KNOW?
- The biggest known snake lived in what is now Egypt about 50 million years ago. It was over 11 m (36 ft) long. Snakes are rarely found as fossils as their fragile skeletons were often broken and scattered.
- The bones that make up the neck are called vertebrae. Humans have 26 vertebrae. *Elasmosaurus* had 76 vertebrae in a neck that was 7 m (23 ft) long.

150 million years ago: *Rhamphorhynchus* alive.
80 million years ago: *Elasmosaurus* alive.

# A changing world

Some reptile species have been remarkably successful at adapting to a changing world. Others, like the dinosaurs, did not succeed in adapting to a new world, and became extinct. During the prehistoric period, creatures evolved and became extinct over millions of years. Today, the rate at which species may become extinct is much faster.

Since humans evolved, reptiles have been killed off in large numbers. Their habitat has been destroyed. The swamps where they live have been drained, the forests cleared, and towns built in their place.

Reptiles have also been hunted and killed because humans are afraid of them. For many years, people have used small animals called mongooses to kill snakes. In some places this has had a disastrous effect on the snake population. The racer snakes of two Caribbean islands were probably made extinct by mongooses, as were two species of tree snake.

c1950  St Croix Tree Snake extinct.
c1960  Jamaican Tree Snake extinct.
c1962  Martinique Racer extinct.
c1973  St Lucia Racer extinct.
c1980  Round Island Boa probably extinct.

◀ The mongoose hunts snakes, killing them with a swift bite behind the head. It can survive the attack of poisonous snakes such as cobras. Mongooses originally lived in Asia and Africa but where they have been introduced onto islands they have had a devastating effect.

## Round Island disaster

Over 100 years ago, in 1844, goats and rabbits were introduced to a tiny island in the Indian Ocean near Mauritius. Round Island is only 1.5 sq km (1 sq mi) in size, and so the newcomers had an enormous effect on the wildlife there. They gradually ate so many of the trees, bushes and grasses that the soil was no longer supported by roots and was easily washed away by the rain.

The vegetation which grew on the island changed, and much of the wildlife was threatened. This included a burrowing snake which scientists do not know very much about.

The Round Island Boa was 1 m (3 ft) long and probably became extinct in 1980 because the topsoil in which it used to live and feed had been washed away.

▼ The Round Island Boa had a pointed head, which helped it burrow through volcanic soil and vegetation.

# Island life

An island provides a unique habitat for the creatures which live on it. The conditions in which these animals live are found only on that particular island, and so the animals develop special features. If natural disasters occur or people come to settle on the island, the native creatures often become extinct.

The Cape Verde Islands are in the Atlantic Ocean, 560 km (348 mi) from the coastline of Senegal in Africa. The tiny islands of Razo and Branco are hot and humid, and are covered in bare rocks and sand. They were once the home of the Cape Verde Giant Skink, a large lizard which fed on seeds, fruits, leaves and the eggs of seabirds. The Cape Verde Giant Skink probably became extinct due to two main causes. Local fishermen hunted the skink, but it was also badly affected by the long droughts which killed the island vegetation. The Cape Verde Giant Skink probably became extinct in about 1940.

A Mediterranean species, the San Stephano Lizard, is thought to have become extinct in 1965. It lived on a small island off Ventotene, to the west of Naples, Italy. The lizard was attacked by disease and hunted by pet cats that had gone wild.

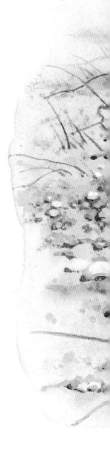

DID YOU KNOW?
- Seven species of lizard have become extinct on the Caribbean islands since 1837.
- Four species of lizard have vanished from Indian Ocean islands since 1650.

c1940 Cape Verde Giant Skink extinct.
c1950 Ratas Island Lizard extinct.
c1965 San Stephano Lizard extinct.

## Destruction of a habitat

The islands of the Mediterranean region were once a haven for all kinds of wildlife, including wild goats, genets, monk seals and migratory birds. In many places, tourist developments, yachting marinas, building and pollution have destroyed the natural habitat. The Ratas Island Lizard became extinct in about 1950. Its small island habitat, off Minorca, was destroyed during the rebuilding of the port of Mahon.

▲ One hundred years ago, the Cape Verde Skink was exhibited in European zoos and studied by scientists. It was a large skink with a body which could measure over 32 mm (12.5 in) in length (not including its tail).

# The Tuatara

The *Rhynchocephalia,* or "beak-heads", were a group of reptiles which appeared on Earth about 200 million years ago. By 100 million years ago, they were mostly extinct. Just one species survives into our own times. It is called the Tuatara, and it lives in New Zealand.

The Tuatara used to live all over New Zealand, but now it is found only on about 30 offshore islands. It is rare and appears on the Red List of threatened animals prepared by the International Union for the Conservation of Nature and Natural Resources (IUCN). It has been protected by law since 1953 and has been bred in captivity in Australia and New Zealand.

The main threat to this ancient reptile comes from hungry Polynesian rats. These rodents are found on seven of the islands where the Tuatara lives. If the Tuatara is to survive, the rats must be prevented from reaching the other islands.

Tuataras feed on grubs, beetles and crickets. They sometimes kill larger animals, such as lizards, frogs and small birds. Although Tuataras are burrowing reptiles, they often shelter in the nesting burrows of seabirds, such as shearwaters and petrels.

▶ The Tuatara can grow up to 70 cm (28 in) long and has a crest of spines running from head to tail. Its feet have sharp claws, and the five toes on each foot are partly joined by webs.

Despite its appearance, the Tuatara is not related to the lizards. Its skull, jaws and backbone are a different shape. The Tuatara can also survive in much lower temperatures than most reptiles. Young Tuatara have a "third eye", a spot between the eyes that reacts to light. This probably helps the young reptile to be aware of how much sunlight it needs to stay warm and active.

DID YOU KNOW?
- The name Tuatara is taken from a Maori word that means "peak-beaked" or crested.
- A Tuatara can lay between 8 and 15 eggs in a clutch. They take up to 15 months to hatch.
- Tuataras are 20 years old before they can breed and they may live to be over 100.

# Snakes at risk

Many creatures are threatened today by changes to their habitat. As chain-saws and flames bring down trees in the vast tropical forests, snakes have been left homeless. As a result some species are thought to have become extinct.

Many people are frightened of snakes, but only 400 of the 2700 species alive today are venomous. Most snakes will attack humans only when they are cornered or threatened. Unfortunately, humans will hunt and kill snakes rather than risk being bitten.

## A vulnerable viper

*Vipera lebetina schweizeri* is a small species of snub-nosed viper that lives on the Cyclades Islands in Greece. In recent years this chain of islands has been developed for tourism and the future of this snake is classified as vulnerable by the IUCN.

▼ *Vipera lebetina schweizeri* measures up to 80 cm (31 in) in length and its body is patterned with reddish-brown markings.

**DID YOU KNOW?**
- Ten million reptile skins are traded each year. Snake skins are used to make belts, wallets, shoes and handbags.
- Many snakes are at risk today in the United States. These include the Ridge-nosed Rattlesnake, three kinds of Garter Snake, two Water Snakes, and the Eastern Indigo Snake.
- Eleven species of viper and rattlesnake are under threat around the world.

▲ The Indian Python lives in the forests of India, Sri Lanka and China. It is listed as vulnerable by the IUCN. If its habitat continues to be cut down and burnt, it may become endangered.

# Lizards

There are about 3000 lizard species alive today, more than any other kind of reptile. Most of these lizards live in countries with a warm or mild climate. About 42 species are thought to be at risk.

Lizards are under threat for many reasons. In Europe, sand dunes and heaths have been destroyed in order to put up buildings. This leaves only small areas where the lizards can live. If a brush fire flares up, the lizards have nowhere to escape to and they may die in their hundreds. Another threat to European lizards is litter. For example, lizards sometimes get trapped in glass bottles that have been thrown away.

Some lizard species lay eggs. Others carry their eggs inside their bodies and give birth to live young. Egg-laying species are particularly at risk. Their eggs may be trampled by humans, dogs and horses, or eaten by rats and mice.

▼ The Gila Monster lives near water in the deserts of Mexico and the south-western United States. It feeds at night on small mammals and eggs, and can grow to 50 cm (20 in) in length. Gila Monsters used to be kept as pets, but they are now protected by law.

## The Komodo Dragon

The world's largest lizard is the Komodo Dragon, which can grow to 3 m (10 ft) in length and weigh up to 136 kg (300 lb). It is very rare and is found only on the islands of Komodo, Rinja and Padar, off the coast of Flores in Indonesia. The Komodo Dragon feeds on monkeys, pigs and deer, and these have been hunted in the past by the islanders. To prevent people killing the Komodo Dragon's only source of food, the islands have been declared a nature reserve.

▲ The Komodo Dragon looks like some of the long-extinct reptiles of prehistoric times. It hunts for its food by day, and hides in rocky areas by night. It has a powerful tail which it can use to defend itself.

# The Hawksbill Turtle

The Hawksbill Turtle is found all around the tropical oceans, from Australia to the Caribbean. Although it is widespread, it is no longer found in very great numbers and is listed by the IUCN as an endangered species. Turtles like the Hawksbill have been killed for thousands of years. The flesh can be eaten and it is a popular meal in the Caribbean, Papua New Guinea and the Solomon Islands.

A greater threat to the turtle has come with the growth of tourism. Turtles are used to make souvenirs. Remote beaches which were once safe places for the females to lay their eggs, can now be reached by jeep and motor boat, and the turtles are easily caught. The turtles are also hunted by divers with spear-guns.

Hawksbill Turtles are now protected by law in many countries, where the export of shells is strictly controlled. However, only a few beaches are protected, or are part of nature reserves. Captive breeding programmes release baby turtles back into the wild and these have been successful in some places.

> **DID YOU KNOW?**
> - Fifty-nine turtle and terrapin species are at risk.
> - Six out of seven species of marine turtle are hunted for their meat, their eggs or their shells.
> - Three million freshwater turtles and terrapins are sold by the pet trade each year.
> - The world's largest marine turtle, the Leatherback, is an endangered species. It can weigh over 450 kg (1000 lb) and measure 1.5 m (5 ft) in length.

◀ The tourist trade is responsible for the death of many turtles, including the Hawksbill Turtle. Turtle shells are polished and then made into souvenirs. Young turtles are stuffed and sold in tourist shops.

▲ The Hawksbill is a medium-sized marine turtle, which takes its name from its bird-like beak. The turtle can weigh up to 75 kg (165 lb) and is about 80 cm (31 in) long.

It lives in shallow, tropical waters and coral reefs, and feeds on weeds, sponges, soft corals and other small creatures.

This Hawksbill Turtle is resting underwater.

The female Hawksbill leaves the sea to lay her eggs. She usually crawls up the beach by night to scoop out a nest in the sand. She lays between 70 and 180 eggs. They take two months to hatch. Then the baby turtles return to the sea. Turtle eggs are often eaten by ghost crabs, lizards and scavenging dogs. Many of the baby turtles are caught by seabirds and lizards as they run down the beach towards the sea.

# Crocodile family

Crocodiles, alligators, caimans and the long-snouted gharials are some of the most impressive reptiles on Earth. With their armour-plated hides, powerful tails and toothy jaws, they look like prehistoric creatures. Unfortunately, many of them may become extinct if action is not taken to save them.

These giant reptiles have been ruthlessly hunted and shot. During this century, 100,000 were killed in Africa alone each year. The hides are used to make shoes and handbags. Some species are killed for sport, or destroyed because they take humans and livestock as prey.

The habitat of alligators and crocodiles has been destroyed in many places by drainage and irrigation schemes. Forests and reedbeds are cleared, and nesting sites are trampled by cattle. Intensive fishing in lakes and rivers has resulted in crocodiles becoming trapped in fishing nets.

> **DID YOU KNOW?**
> ● Fourteen species of crocodile and one species of gharial are threatened with extinction. Four species of alligator and caiman are also at risk.
> ● The largest reptile on Earth, the Estuarine or Saltwater Crocodile, is an endangered species.

The little Yangtze Alligator is about 2 m (7 ft) long and lives in China, in the muddy water of the lower Chang Jiang River. It was once found over a much wider area, but today it is an endangered species.

This alligator sleeps, or hibernates, during the winter months. As people have cleared land, the muddy banks where it burrows and nests have been disturbed. The Yangtze Alligator is now protected by law and has been bred in special reserves.

Today, the hunting of crocodiles and alligators and the sale of their skins are strictly controlled in many countries. Game reserves are playing an important part in protecting some species. Crocodile farms hatch eggs and breed the reptiles in captivity. Even so, the danger to these magnificent creatures continues.

## The Black Caiman

A hundred years ago, the caiman was common around the Amazon River and other, smaller rivers of the South American rain forests. About 60 years ago, hunters came to the region in search of skins. Black Caimans were killed in their millions. The destruction of their habitat for farming has meant that many local populations of caimans have become extinct. Black Caimans have been successfully bred in captivity, but the future of the whole species is in danger.

▼ The Black Caiman is the biggest member of the alligator family in the Americas. It is up to 6 m (20 ft) in length and hunts other reptiles, pigs, deer, fish and large rodents called capybaras.

# Providing protection

The Mugger, or Marsh Crocodile, is a broad-snouted reptile with powerful jaws. It is still found in Sri Lanka, India and Nepal, but in the last 40 years its numbers have declined drastically in Bangladesh, and it may already be extinct there. It is very rare in Pakistan, where it is already listed as endangered, and is barely surviving in Iran.

In the past, the mugger was hunted for its skin and meat, and in some places its teeth and bones were used to make medicines. Today, the main threat to the survival of the mugger is from fishermen protecting their nets. Muggers which become entangled in the nets are normally killed immediately.

The mugger's habitat is also being destroyed. Forests have been cleared and swamps drained. Where reservoirs have been built they have often been stocked with fish. The reservoirs could provide homes for the crocodiles, but wandering muggers are often destroyed in order to protect the fish.

Young gharials at the Royal Chitwan National Park in Nepal. A gharial breeding project was started here in 1978, because fewer than 100 gharials survived in Nepal. By 1981, young gharials were being released into the wild.

Gharials were once common in fast-flowing rivers in India and neighbouring countries. They have been hunted for their skin, their eggs have been stolen and their habitat has been destroyed. Gharials are now endangered and their survival depends on breeding schemes.

PROTECTING THE MUGGERS
- Many Indian states have set up sanctuaries where muggers are protected.
- In India, eggs have been collected and young muggers bred in captivity in zoos at Jaipur, Ahmedabad, Hyderabad and Baroda. Muggers have been released into the wild, where they have bred successfully.
- The World Wide Fund for Nature has helped to set up a "Crocodile Bank" in Madras, India, to breed muggers and carry out research.

▲ The mugger rarely exceeds 4 m (13 ft) in length. It lives in rivers, lakes, pools and reservoirs, and feeds on fish, waterfowl and small mammals.

The laws protecting the muggers need to be enforced more strongly, particularly where muggers are in danger from poachers.

# Saving the reptiles

People are gradually beginning to realize that reptiles are among the most fascinating creatures on our planet. Many reptiles perform useful tasks. When the numbers of Black Caiman declined in South America, a lot of farms and small towns were overrun by rodents because the caimans were no longer eating them.

Scientists are working hard for the future, breeding reptiles and releasing them into the wild. However, the trade in skins and tortoiseshell has to be stopped.

▼ These lizards were crated and exported for the pet trade. They died during the journey. Many endangered reptile species are transported, illegally and cruelly. Laws are not enforced. The international trade in endangered species is worth billions of dollars each year.

There are laws to control hunting, but it is difficult to catch the people who break the laws. People must be persuaded not to buy goods which involve the death of so many reptiles each year. The pet trade must also be stopped from relying on animals captured in the wild.

The greatest risk to reptiles comes from loss of habitat. The destruction of wetlands and forests is a problem that affects not just reptiles, but humans too. The whole balance of life on our planet depends on humans caring for the environment.

▲ A Thai girl holds a python. Snakes are not the slimy creatures of nightmares. They are dry to the touch and mostly harmless if handled correctly. It is important that people learn to overcome their fear of reptiles and try to understand their way of life.

# Glossary

**amphibian** An animal which has evolved so that part of its life is spent in the water and part on land.

**cold-blooded** Unable to control its own body temperature. Reptiles are cold-blooded. Their body heat changes with the temperature of their surroundings.

**dinosaur** One of a group of reptiles which lived on Earth long ago. They became extinct 65 million years ago.

**endangered** At risk of becoming extinct.

**environment** The world in which a plant or animal lives, including the soil, climate, vegetation and air.

**evolve** To develop or adapt over a long period. Animals evolve into new forms over many millions of years.

**extinct** Having disappeared, died out. Scientists now declare a creature to be extinct when it has not been seen in the wild for 50 years.

**fossil** The remains of an ancient animal or plant preserved in rock.

**habitat** The place in which a particular animal or plant lives.

**hibernate** To sleep through the winter, or coldest, months of the year.

**introduce** To bring a creature to live in an area where it does not occur naturally.

**nature reserve** An area of land where wild animals are protected by law.

**rare** Few in number. Rare reptiles are not necessarily in danger, but they obviously run a higher risk than other animals.

**reptile** A cold-blooded, egg-laying animal whose body is covered in scales.

**rodent** Any small, gnawing mammal such as a rat or mouse.

**species** A single group of identical animals or plants.

**venomous** Full of or containing poison. Certain snakes inject poison into a victim through a bite.

**vulnerable** Of a species, likely to become endangered if action is not taken to halt its decline in numbers.

# Find out more

- The study of reptiles and amphibians is called herpetology. It is a fascinating hobby. The British Isles are on the edge of Europe's milder weather zones, and so form the northernmost limit of the range of some reptiles. Rare British species include the Sand Lizard and the Smooth Snake. In the Channel Islands you may even see the Green Lizard and the Common Wall Lizard. Species you are more likely to come across in Britain include the Common Lizard, the Grass Snake, the venomous Adder and the Slow Worm, which is a legless lizard.

- Dinosaurs may be seen today – in a museum. Many big cities have a Museum of Natural History or a Science Museum, where you can see fossils and reconstructions of the great prehistoric reptiles and their skeletons. The Natural History section of the British Museum is in Cromwell Road, London.

- The best place to see tropical reptiles, if not in their native habitat, is in a zoo. Find out if the zoo is helping to breed any endangered reptile species.

- Are you interested in helping to protect endangered reptiles around the world? The World Wide Fund for Nature has a junior membership. Contact Panda House, Weyside Park, Catteshall Lane, Godalming, Surrey GU7 1XR, for details of regional activities.

- Throughout England, Scotland, Wales and Ireland there are local nature clubs and conservation trusts which organize activities and help protect nature reserves.

# Time chart

| PREHISTORIC PERIOD | | |
|---|---|---|
| **Years ago** | **Human history** | **Natural history** |
| 340 million | | First reptiles evolve. |
| 280 million | | Reptiles roam the Earth. |
| 150 million | | *Rhamphorhynchus* alive. |
| 80 million | | *Elasmosaurus* alive. |
| 75 million | | *Tyrannosaurus rex* alive. |
| 65 million | | Dinosaurs become extinct. |
| 50 million | | Largest known prehistoric snake alive. |
| 12 million | | Largest known prehistoric tortoise alive. |
| 4 million | "Ape-people", such as *Australopithecus,* evolve. | |
| 100,000 | Modern people evolve, hunters with weapons of stone. They kill reptiles, fish, mammals and birds. | |
| **HISTORIC PERIOD** | | |
| 10,000-1500BC | Humans in Middle East learn to farm. Reptiles hunted for food or killed as pests. Snakes considered sacred in many regions, including ancient Egypt, Crete and India. | Changes in climate and vegetation. |
| 1500BC-AD800 | Classical period in Europe, followed by so-called Dark Ages. The sacred writings of Jews, Christians and Muslims condemn snakes as "evil". Reptiles hunted. | Loss of habitat. |
| 800-1700 | European settlement overseas. Rats, cats and pigs introduced to small islands. These prey upon native reptiles. | Two species of Giant Tortoise (1700) and one Giant Skink (1650) extinct on Mauritius. |
| 1700-1800 | European settlement overseas. Beginnings of industry. Clearance of forests, drainage of wetlands. | Two species of Giant Tortoise extinct on Réunion (1760-1773), and two on Rodriguez (1795). Loss of habitat. |
| 1800-1900 | European settlement overseas. Spread of Mongoose, predator of reptiles. Building of cities, industrial pollution. Growth of interest in natural history and evolution. | Martinique Lizard extinct (1837). Night Gecko extinct on Rodriguez (1841). Two species of Giant Tortoise extinct on the Galapagos Islands (1876-1890). Réunion Skink extinct (1880). Jamaican Giant Galliwasp extinct (1880). |
| 1900- | Spread of towns and industry. Pollution. Destruction of rain forests. Drainage of wetlands. Growth of interest in conservation. Attempts to control trade in reptile skins. | Marion's Giant Tortoise extinct on Seychelles (1918); two species extinct on Galapagos (1906 and 1957). Day Gecko extinct on Rodriguez (1920). Five Caribbean lizards and four Caribbean snakes probably extinct. Boa probably extinct on Round Island (1980?). Over 180 species listed as being at risk by the IUCN. |

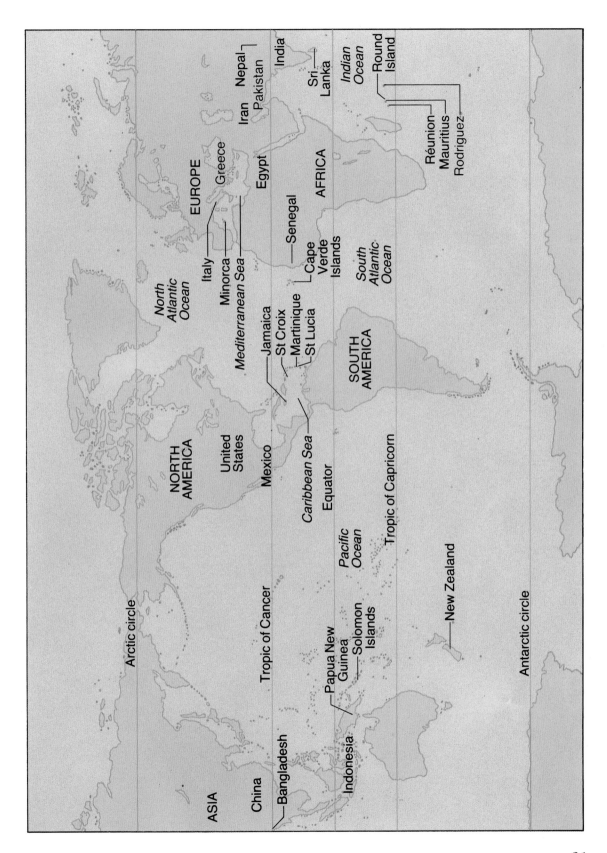

31

# Index